DEALING WITH AN INSECURE BOYFRIEND

Finding Happiness with a Guy Who's Insecure

EMILY WALKER

INTRODUCTION

What an incredible feeling it is to meet a guy who values you and treats you like you're the most important woman in the world to him. You feel cherished and loved, especially if you've only dated insensitive and narcissistic men in the past. But what if this man you think is Mr. Right turns out to be just like all the other men you've dated in the past? Or worse? Because the beginning of a relationship with an insecure man is rather rosy.

Initially, you'll be showered with gifts, compliments, and so much love that you will feel on top of the world. You may believe you are the luckiest girl alive. You won't just feel it; you'll know it. However, what usually happens is that after a few weeks, his affection for you turns into an obsession.

He demands your undivided attention and expects you to constantly prove your love for him. From texting him all day to paying attention to him every time he says your name, you'll be expected to constantly smother him with love because he never stops asking for it. It can be exhausting and frustrating to constantly prove your love to your insecure boyfriend.

You will also be introduced to his mind games over time. Mind games are difficult to deal with when dating an insecure man, so watch out because things are about to get really bumpy. An emotionally insecure guy can be a dating nightmare, leaving you wondering how to deal with an insecure man. But that doesn't mean your relationship is doomed. If you truly love him, there are ways to deal with his insecurity and possibly even help him break his pattern of needy, clingy behavior.

Dating an Insecure Man – The Relationship Dynamic

Is it worth dating insecure men? Dating an insecure man can make the dating experience extremely unpleasant. Constant fighting, silly relationship squabbles, trying to understand each other's moods... and it's all because he doesn't believe where you were last night. This can become exhausting and will eventually have an impact on your mental health.

He is overprotective, possessive, and easily jealous; he has low self-esteem and even believes he is unworthy of your love. And this is why, when you are not around, he doesn't take a second to switch his mood, accuse you, or even bombard you with calls and messages. His internal turmoil spills all over the relationship. Every now and then, you may find yourself saying, "I'm just so tired of my boyfriend being insecure."

When you first started dating, it might have seemed cute when your insecure boyfriend kept asking you what you were up to or who you were hanging out with. You probably liked the fact that he was so involved in your life, showing you so much concern, not realizing that you were dealing with an insecure partner.

However, as time passed and his true colors began to emerge, it was only natural for you to become irritated by the fact that he constantly expects you to be answerable to him. Most of your major fights have most likely been caused by you missing his calls or failing to respond to his texts in a timely manner.

You'll never know what's going on in the mind of an insecure boyfriend. One moment, he can make you feel so important and special that he would steal the moon and stars for you. But at other times, he may make you feel suffocated in the relationship. The question of how to deal with an insecure man then becomes all-consuming, consuming most of your mental space and energy.

Dominant Characteristics of an Insecure Man

Before you shout, "My man is insecure and it is ruining our relationship!" consider the following traits of an insecure man. Yes, you may be dating an insecure man. However, with the following pointers, we will be certain:

- **He is controlling:** Such a man is known for his manipulative and controlling behavior.

He'll want to control what you wear, who you meet, who you talk to, and so on.

- **He gets jealous easily:** A jealous boyfriend is the most obvious sign that you are dating an insecure man. He will be triggered by your seemingly harmless interactions with any person of the sex you are romantically/sexually attracted to and may even lash out at you.
- **Low confidence:** His level of confidence is extremely low. He is constantly doubting himself and seeks your validation. He is overly concerned with what others think of him and his life, and he constantly feels the need to compete with others.
- **He is emotionally sensitive:** One of the difficulties in dating an insecure man is that he is highly sensitive and easily upset. You will constantly find him venting his rage on you for trivial matters or getting hurt over the non-issues.

- **He brags:** Dating someone with insecurities entails putting up with their show-off attitude at all times. He will enjoy bragging about himself to hide his flaws. This is a defense mechanism he employs to hide his insecurities.

- **Belittling you:** Bullying and belittling you will become a routine for him. He will constantly criticize you and mock your friends. He does that to feel better about himself.

- **He can't take criticism well:** Criticism is something that an insecure man will not tolerate. If you point out his flaws, he will become enraged and may even throw a fit if you make a harmless joke about him.

- **He is skeptical:** He will always be suspicious of others' intentions and will be unable to trust anyone, including you.

Telltale Signs You're Dating an Insecure Man

Insecurity is a personality trait that has the potential to derail any healthy relationship. It can cause a lot of tension and lead to a lot of unresolved issues between the two of you. At the start of the relationship, you may feel that your boyfriend is perfect because he cares so much about you.

But soon, that insecurity rears its ugly head, and then you realize you're in a relationship with someone who has massive and unreasonable expectations of and from you. 'Intense' and 'draining' are only two words that begin to describe the experience of dating an insecure man.

If you concur with the following signs, you have every reason to say, "My boyfriend is insecure." To be certain, it's a good idea to understand the signs you're dating an insecure man so you know exactly what you're dealing with. Prepare yourself because this is a lengthy list.

1) He devotes all of his time to you.

He hardly has any friends or interesting hobbies to keep him busy. His world revolves solely around you, which can become quite smothering for you. "I'm sick of my man's insecurity and clinginess." If your man's presence causes you to feel this way because he doesn't have a life outside of the relationship, you can be fairly certain that his insecurities get the best of him more often than not.

2) He controls all aspect of your life

Instead of respecting your opinions and giving you space, he becomes an insecure boyfriend who controls every aspect of your life. He wants you to do everything his way, from what you say to how you dress. Dealing with an insecure partner can be suffocating, and you may feel as if you're losing yourself in order to keep him happy and your relationship afloat.

3) He keeps telling you to keep things as simple as possible.

He constantly asks you to dress down because he is either insecure about his own appearance in comparison to you or he doesn't want anyone else ogling you. If he can't handle his partner getting a bit of attention or even a compliment from someone, he's got a lot of emotional baggage to deal with. That emotional baggage is spilling onto your partnership in the form of his insecurity.

4) Jealousy is second nature to him.

Jealousy and insecure men go hand in hand. He is jealous not just of your male friends, but also of any man who tries to come close to you. If you have close relationships with your girlfriends, he doesn't like it either. If you buy them presents or go out of your way to do things for them, he gets angry.

5) He puts you down

Dating someone who is insecure looks something like this: An insecure boyfriend will make you feel small and will fail to empower you. He will have a problem with everything you do, which will become very frustrating for you over time. Instead of being your biggest cheerleader, he will make you feel bad about yourself. In the long run, a relationship with an insecure man can severely damage your self-esteem and confidence.

6) He is constantly keeping an eye on you.

He will constantly monitor you and want to know where you are, what you're doing, and who you're hanging out with. So be prepared for him to begin texting or calling you incessantly when you go out with your friends. It's no surprise that you struggled with the "sick of my boyfriend being insecure" feeling more often than not. Catering to all his emotional needs can feel like a full-time job.

7) He never admits his mistakes.

If he makes a mistake, you will notice that he will begin to blame you or someone else for his mistakes. But he will never admit to his own mistakes. Insecure men find it difficult to say things like "I'm sorry, I messed up" or "This was my fault." They have an overwhelming need to present an infallible exterior because their self-esteem is already battered. Even if it is founded on lies, half-truths, or pure gaslighting.

8) **He loves to hear compliments but no feedback.**

He will gladly accept compliments from you because they will boost his low self-esteem. However, he will not appreciate any feedback or constructive criticism from you. If you tell him he needs to change his behavior or suggest that he work on certain personality traits, you will most likely be met with a cold shoulder and some stonewalling.

9) **Your loyalty is doubted**

He is always suspicious of your motives and uses mind games to test your loyalty, and you may not even realize it. One of the most obvious signs that you're dealing with an insecure partner is if he accuses you of cheating on him or implies that you're pursuing other romantic interests while in a relationship with him.

10) **If things do not go his way, he becomes aggressive.**

When you confront him, his angry outbursts become common, and he becomes aggressive. Fights with him can turn ugly. Any deviation from the expected behavior from you can set off his temper tantrums. Even if you have done nothing to warrant an apology or explanation, you will find yourself justifying your actions to him.

And now that we've established that you are indeed dating an insecure man, it's time to look into how to deal with the situation. Recognizing this relationship problem is the first step, so congratulations. But what now? Continue reading.

Dealing With an Insecure Boyfriend

Insecurity is not something that can be easily cured or done away with. It will take effort, time, patience, and introspection from both you and your boyfriend to pull him out of this mess. You might even have a depressed boyfriend on your hands, which could make matters much worse. However, if you put forth the effort, you can assist your insecure boyfriend in overcoming his insecurity.

But he must also be willing to accept your assistance and work to improve himself. It is even possible that he will require professional help. But, for the time being, here are 16 things you can do to help him.

1. **Evaluate your own behavior and conduct in the relationship.**

Sounds frustrating because all this time you've felt like he's been hurting you and it almost sounds unfair that you have to check your own self. But you have to for love. It is time to be the bigger person here. You must examine your interactions with your insecure boyfriend.

Do you give him enough time and attention? Have you been unfaithful to your partner or flirted with other men? It's time to make certain that your actions are not the cause of his increased insecurity. You may mean well, but there may be something about your behavior that is ticking him off. If you can find it and fix it, you've already won half the battle. Something in the relationship may be causing your boyfriend's insecurity.

If he does not exhibit any signs of insecurity in his interactions with other people or other aspects of his life, then you must reconsider whether your actions are causing him to act in this manner and making your relationship toxic. Perhaps he doesn't feel worthy of you or doesn't get enough validation from you. These things could be causing him to feel insecure.

2. **Extend your understanding and support to him**

Genevieve Bachman, an interior designer, once told us that her man was extremely controlling and demanded that he choose her outfits for her every morning. He would continuously text her while she was at work and would ask her to sit alone during lunch and speak to him over the phone.

"I learned the hard way that dealing with an insecure man is tough. Colin was always glued to me, trying to exert control over aspects of my life that were truly none of his business. All of that ended when I sat him down and discussed the issues with him. "Things didn't get tremendously better, but once he realized I loved him, he backed off a little," she stated.

If you want your partner to overcome his insecurity, you must communicate with him and eliminate all of his concerns and doubts. Remember that you are dealing with an immature man at all times. So be mindful of your words and try to be as kind as possible. Keep the promises you made to him and try to live up to his expectations, if you believe they are reasonable.

3. Show him that you care

Connie Jensen told us a similar experience about herself when she began dating an insecure man. "Ricardo would often get mad when I went to office parties or stayed out late with my friends," she said. He even threw tantrums if I arrived home late from work. He kept doubting me and accusing me of having an office romance that I wasn't telling him about."

When they sat down and talked openly, she realized that his problems stemmed from her boss, who was known to have a negative reputation when it comes to his female employees.

She made it clear that she wasn't okay with him having a problem with the way she dressed and attended office parties. It took him a while to recognize how badly this was affecting her, but he eventually made a concerted effort, and their relationship is now stronger than ever. Sometimes the solution to how to deal with an insecure man can be as simple as not dismissing his fears as a result of his insecurity and listening to him with an open mind.

4. **Make him understand the importance he has in your life.**

Make an effort to show your insecure boyfriend how much you value him. He needs it more than you think. Make him understand that he is irreplaceable in your life and that you care for him in the same way you have been doing all this time.

This will reassure him, and he may realize his insecurity is baseless or that he is just overthinking it.

You don't have to spend extravagantly to do this. Little romantic gestures, such as getting him his favorite food, ought to do the trick. You can also emphasize that he is loved and valued in the relationship by getting him small, but thoughtful, gifts from time to time. You should know how to treat him properly.

If you're browsing an online store and come across a quirky beer mug that you know your boyfriend will like, simply order it for him and give it to him on your next date. Or, if you see a shirt or scarf that you know will look good on him, don't put it off until a special occasion. These gestures can help reassure him that he is always on your mind and alleviate his insecurities.

5. **Encourage him to talk about his past with you**

Your boyfriend's insecurity issues could be the result of past experiences or hurt caused to him in previous relationships. Encourage him to talk about his past experiences in order to get to the root of the problem, which could stem from a previous relationship or even toxic parenting in his childhood.

If his behavior is linked to his upbringing, we recommend that he seek professional help and consult with a therapist. Childhood issues can become deeply ingrained in a person's psyche, necessitating therapy to address. You should consider discussing this with your boyfriend, especially if he had a difficult childhood or issues with abandonment.

It is not always easy to deal with an insecure partner. It may sometimes entail nudging him to delve deeper into his triggers and emotional baggage. That can be difficult for someone who has been carrying around years of bottled-up hurt, anger, or trauma. So many people live their lives actively attempting to avoid confronting their emotions. So you have a lot of work ahead of you.

6. **Try not to become like your insecure boyfriend.**

Just because your boyfriend is insecure, doesn't mean that you should become jealous and insecure as well. Behaving like your insecure boyfriend will only lead to more problems in your relationship, so don't go down that road! Avoid the temptation to give him a taste of his own medicine. It is a recipe for disaster, making your relationship even more toxic and dysfunctional.

You will destroy your relationship with your boyfriend if you also start to embrace his thought process. You may feel tempted to give him a taste of his own medicine, but doing so will only breed hatred between you and quickly turn the relationship sour. Help him, don't punch back at him.

7. You must completely avoid lying to them

Try to be as truthful as possible in the relationship, because if you lie to him, his trust will be broken and his insecurities will grow exponentially. If he already has trust issues, instead of giving him reasons to feed that, work with him to help him live a happy and loving life. With his thought process, he's probably always looking for those. So stay in the clear, that way you can both be happy.

If you lie to him and he discovers it, you will only add fuel to the fire. Your insecure boyfriend already has obvious trust issues, and being dishonest will make him even more paranoid and skeptical of you. Be truthful to yourself and to him. Do this not only to appease him, but also to build a happy and lasting relationship.

8. **Make plans with your friends that also include him.**

One of the difficulties in dating an insecure man is that they do not trust your friends or other people you hang out with. Is there a way to make him do away with such frivolous concerns? If you know that going out with your friends, particularly your male friends, upsets your insecure boyfriend, make plans with them that involve him. That way, he can meet them, get to know them, and finally get rid of his suspicions.

Sometimes the fear of the unknown is far worse than the reality. Who knows, when he meets your friends, he might just fall in love with them and realize he has nothing to worry about. When he observes your platonic interactions and develops a rapport with your friends, he will lower his guard and become more trusting of both you and them. This will be beneficial in the long run because everyone wants their friends to get along with their significant other, right?

9. **Express your concerns and insecurities to him.**

To deal with an insecure partner in a relationship, it's time that you also let your own guard down. When you share your insecurities with your man, he will gain the confidence to express his concerns to you. This mutual sharing of doubts and fears will strengthen your bond more than ever.

The foundation of any healthy relationship is being open and honest with each other. Open communication means that you are both comfortable with each other and are not afraid to show your vulnerable side in each other's company. Isn't that the essence of true love? You must encourage each other to discuss and share your problems and fears.

10. Give them time to improve

Your insecure boyfriend will not change overnight. Giving him the time and space he needs to deal with his insecurities is the best thing you can do. When dating an insecure man, be patient and do not rush the process. This does not, however, imply that you tolerate his abusive behavior.

If you don't see any signs of improvement, consider this one of the major relationship red flags and end the relationship. Staying in a relationship with someone who refuses to grow as a human being and is stuck in his old ways is bad for you and your mental health. You deserve much more than that. You can only do so much to strengthen your relationship; he needs to also meet you halfway.

11. Consult with a therapist

Counseling has many advantages, so if you and your boyfriend want to seek help, it may be beneficial to speak with a therapist. A therapist can help you reconnect while also working through your boyfriend's insecurity issues. Thus, enlisting the assistance of one would be beneficial to both your boyfriend and you. If your boyfriend suggests it, it is a positive sign that he wants to improve himself and recognizes there is a problem that needs to be addressed.

Make sure you encourage him and assist him in finding a good therapist to help him deal with his issues. You may try your hardest to figure out how to deal with an insecure man and save your relationship, but you may lack the necessary knowledge and skills to assist him in overcoming his issues. This is why encouraging him to seek professional help is your best option for resolving the problem.

12. Compliment him now and again

Dating an insecure man means dating a man with low self-esteem. If you compliment him on a regular basis, you will have the opportunity to help him see himself more positively. Just be as smooth and genuine as possible when complimenting him to help boost his self-esteem. It must be credible in order to work.

Perhaps something at work or with his family is causing him to doubt his own worth, and your kind words will help him rebuild his self-esteem. A simple "I'm so proud of you today" or "I love it when you do that for your sister" can go a long way toward making him feel recognized. It never hurts to make your significant other feel special every now and then, as this will uplift their mood and self-confidence.

13. Watch what you say

How do you have a relationship with an insecure man? Try not to say anything that will cause your boyfriend unnecessary pain. Yes, if you are in the middle of a heated argument, you should present your arguments, but try to remain calm and avoid hitting him where it hurts. You don't have to change yourself; simply be mindful so that you don't upset him unnecessarily. Work with him progressively and take him into confidence.

Do not be afraid to seek his advice on certain issues. If you want to upgrade your wardrobe or are simply in the mood for some shopping, ask your boyfriend for his thoughts on dresses, shoes, and accessories.

If you are at home and doing this online, it can be a fun way to pass the time and get to know each other's tastes a little better. He will feel important to you, which will help you gauge what he is comfortable with. You must remember, however, that you have the final say because it is your life and you cannot let him walk all over you.

14. Be a good listener to him

To understand him, you must learn to be a good listener. Listening intently can help a relationship thrive. When he rants about things he is insecure about, he needs to know that you are truly there for him and are listening to his concerns. That's the only way he will be able to let go of everything that is bothering him.

Sometimes a simple rant about something seemingly insignificant can reveal an underlying issue that is causing him to act in a certain way. So , you must listen to him when he is upset or going through a difficult time in order to better understand him and strengthen your relationship.

15. Don't joke about his insecurities

You must avoid making light of his insecurities, whether in public or in private. Avoid publicly criticizing him or making a joke in front of all your friends. You must respect him and avoid hurting him at all costs. Remember that you are not only dealing with an insecure partner, but also with a man who has low self-esteem. And exposing his vulnerabilities will do more harm than good.

Joy and Hunter were out to dinner with their friends once. Hunter had recently gained a few pounds due to work-related stress, and he felt uncomfortable in his own skin. He'd told Joy about it openly, and yet when his friends poked his belly and laughed, Joy jumped on board and laughed with them. Hunter felt violated and struggled to trust her again. Needless to say, their sex life also became non-existent after this because he felt so self-conscious around her.

16. Encourage them to socialize

If you're wondering, "How do I get my insecure boyfriend to open up?" we recommend encouraging him to socialize. Being surrounded by positive people will enable him to grow and become a better person. Encourage him to socialize with genuine people who care about him.

As he realizes how much happiness and love awaits him out there, he may be able to let go of the negative thoughts he has been holding onto. This change will not happen overnight, but he can get there with consistent effort and a dedication to breaking negative thought patterns and substituting them with positive thoughts. Your role in all of this is to assist him in staying on track and not becoming discouraged by minor setbacks along the way.

Dating an insecure man does not mean the end of your relationship. You just need to be wise, kind, and patient so that the insecurity does not worsen over time.

www.ingramcontent.com/pod-product-compliance
Lightning Source LLC
LaVergne TN
LVHW020540160826
845677LV00015B/4147

* 9 7 9 8 3 6 7 0 4 0 4 3 2 *